DEATH - AN ULTIMATE TRUTH

MEGHA AGARWAL

Made with ♥ on the Notion Press Platform
www.notionpress.com

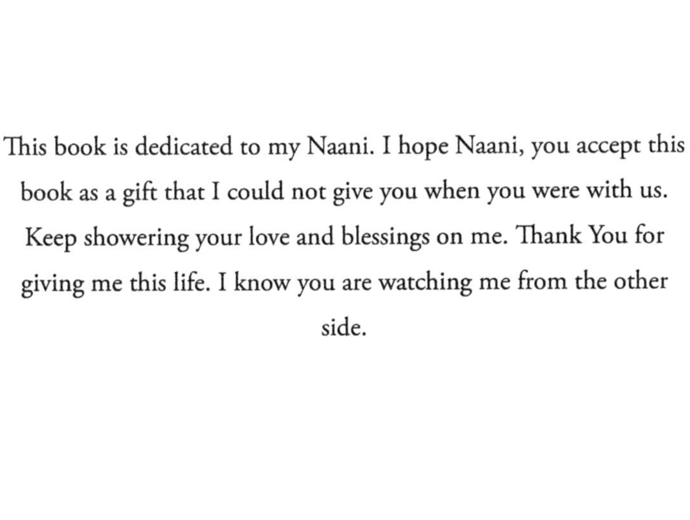

This book is dedicated to my Naani. I hope Naani, you accept this book as a gift that I could not give you when you were with us. Keep showering your love and blessings on me. Thank You for giving me this life. I know you are watching me from the other side.

Contents

Preface *vii*

Prologue *ix*

1. Death - An Ultimate Truth 1

2. A Young Death 3

Part 1

3. Waqt Se Phele 7

Part 2

4. Death Of Relationships 11

Part 3

5. Dum Taudtey Rishtey 15

Part 4

6. Dying In Arms Of Stranger 19

Part 5

7. Wo Mera Apna Shehar 23

Part 6

8. Your Remembrance 27

Part 7

9. Kaisi Yaad Banenge Hum 31

Part 8

10. Thought For After Death 35

Part 9

11. Aisa Kyu Ho Raha Hai? 39

Part 10

12. Death Of A Soilder 43

Contents

Part 11

13. Ek Maut Aisi Bhi 47

Part 12

Treat For The Shayari Lovers 51

Preface

As a reader, you must be wondering why I choose Death as the topic of my first-ever book. As they say, "**har ant k baad ek nayi shuruat hoti hai**" and death is the ultimate destination of all humans. But, this book will be the beginning of my life as an author. I often heard that one should not talk about death on happy occasions and I want to remove that stigma. I want to begin my new life journey by sharing some beautiful poems on Death.

Tried to justify both English and Hindi poems followed by a Sher to take you on the long drive of poetry.

Prologue

Death is considered a very inauspicious topic in my surroundings. It is unpleasant to talk about death, stand close to dead bodies or visit the Manikarnika Ghat (holiest cremation ground) of Banaras.

I don't understand why we run away in the opposite direction when we need to face the ultimate truth of life. Is it human nature to maintain distance from the process that we can't control?

Why don't we want to explore more about our ultimate truth of life? Why is it inauspicious to talk about death? All these questions inspired me to write the following poetries.

Also, I want to remove the negative feelings associated with death. Death is indeed our ultimate destination, but we often tend to forget that and never talk about it with anyone.

What changed my perspective on Death?

I lost my Naani which gave my family a huge shock as we were not expecting or ready to say goodbye so early. And suddenly I felt like I would have hugged her last time and be thankful for all the blessings she showered on her grandchildren.

Fast forward to 6 months later, I found this book on my bookshelf - Death by Sadhguru. Always fantasizing about life after death, I started reading this book. The book began with the acceptance of Death as the ultimate truth of our life. A person who always believes in living her life to the fullest, the initial chapter of this book made me realize how to live every second of life as one day everyone is gonna die. And also, helped me to channel the grief of losing my Naani by accepting the truth that she is gone and she is now in a better place.

Without mourning even for a second, let's dive into the Death of people, emotions, and relationships.

"Khauf-e-maut khaye betha hai wo,

Jindagi jeena bhulakar"

1. Death - An Ultimate Truth

Resourced : Google

One day I am going to die,

I accept this truth, no deny.
I will be lying under the tomb,
There will be no emotions and wound
My graveyard will be like the new building in the city
Funny it is, I am still talking materialistic - as I am greedy
My loved ones are going to visit me some days
Here I will be with my new family from a different country and estate
I might miss all the food and fun here,
But I'll be free from the duty and the pity
I will meet the ultimate truth of life,
Where I and death will bitch about the lie(life)
I and my fellow dead people will cheer each other,
And we are going to think, what's next after this weather gets clear?
Who'll answer all the doubts we'll have,
I am already worried if things will be alright after my demise,
Leave it I have done enough, now it is not my time to sacrifice.
I have lived enough for the love, expectations, and care of people,
It is the time to have fun and roam around the city like a ripper
Goodbye to all the living organisms,
Don't laugh at others' death, as your cessation is near.

2. A Young Death

Don't calculate my experience from my fossils,
I died younger.
A long ago before the body.
Yet, my teeth and bones gonna tell a different story.
Here I am screaming loud
Hear my tale from my mouth
There was the burden of expectations
Have tried to escape
Had drouth and land was bare
No one heard my story when I was alive
Don't give the attention now,
I feel despise
You must be thinking I have seen nothing
As I died younger
it was a curse, not a blessing
Leave me with my half-broken ankle
And two missing teeth
If you can't ignore
Throw me in the seethe!

Resourced : Google

3. Waqt Se Phele

Mere gujarne se phele, mere sapno ka janaja nikal chuka tha,
Asal mein bhoj jimmedariyon ka itna tha,
Ki bachpane mein hee bado jitni chinta
Or bujargo jitni samjdhari aane lagi thee
Manna mere jism ne kuch or dastan sunayi hogi,
Par isse kahan meri jindagi ki ajmaaish hogi
Sharir ki haddion k tootne ka bhi gum utna na tha
Par jindagi ne jo reed ki haddi todi
Uska gum meri kabar mein mere saath jaane tak
Mere andar hee dafan raha!

"Jindagi ne umar se phele bahut kuch sikha diya,

Dikhne mein bacha hee tha

Par mere tajurbe or jimmedariyo ne

Mujhe mere bade hone ka ehsaas

Waqt se bahut phele kara diya

Yeh mann kuch or hee dastaan sunata raha,

Par mere tajurbe ne,

Meri shaksiyat ko bahut phele dafna diya"

4. Death of Relationships

I don't want you to stand by my deathbed
All I ever wanted you to fill our relationship gap
Don't let this toxicity crap spread
No more chances already gave you enough lap
Don't let those tears from eyes shed
Haven't you noticed all the red flags
I was used by you like a doormat
I am done being a stupid Acrobat!
I wanted you to be closest to me when I was alive
But you choose to hold on to that - one night
A night when I lost my mind, you lost control over your mouth
We fought, screamed, and blamed each other for everything from North to South
My ego swallowed and created this distance
Maybe your self-respect also asked you to forget my existence
But, here we are today at my cremation
Neither I can ignore you over your face
Nor you can turn your back
To avoid the uncomfortable gaze
Why are you crying?
Now, when I am gone
You could have become a person with a big heart

When we were going through storm
No worries!
I am happy that you are here
Forgiving me for all the wear-tear
Hope, the rest of life you will remember me
For my good words and deeds
I still wish you were there in my time of need.

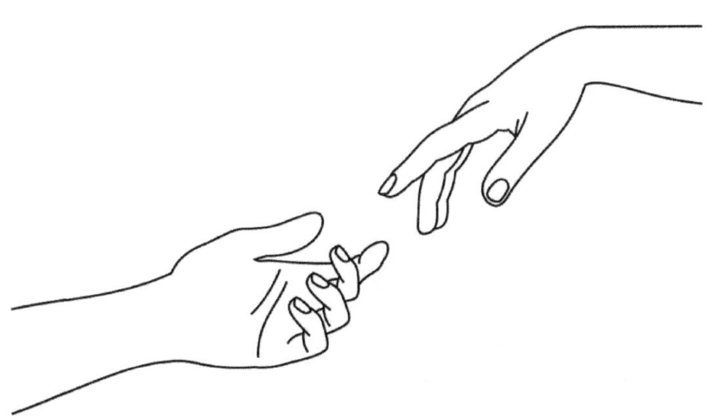

Resourced : Google

5. Dum Taudtey Rishtey

Kehte theh khudko rishte sambhal lo,
Kuch jamane ki akad ne
Toh kuch mere aham ne,
Mujhe inki ahmiyat ka ilam na hone diya!
Mein jinn logo se durr-durr bhagti rahi
Kya unka mere saath rishta hokar bhi,
Durr rehna, mere taqdeer ka ek hissa raha?
Haa khushi hai jo tum mere janaje pe aaye ho
Par humare rishte ki jab maut huyi thee tumne toh uff tak nahi ki
Toh aaj mein tumpe ranj rakhu, Ya shukar manau?
Ki tumne aaj bhi arso phele kiya wo ek waada "tere janaje pe jarur khada milunga"
Mein jinda nahi hun, par jo bhi hai dekho na, aaj apne saath hai
Tumara jindagi bhar saath na hone ka gum liye jaa rahe hai hum,
Kal tak mein tumari aankho mein khatak rahi theh,
Aaj tumare aankhon se ashq behke beh rahe hai,
Kyu mujhe itni badi keemat chukani padi,
Tumhe apne pass bulane k liye?
Apne aapko acha banane k liye?

Kya yahi jindagi ka dastur hai?
Ya hum theh jiska yeh fitoor tha?

"Chala gaya mein ek pachtava leke iss duniya se,

Galti tumari thee ya meri,

Gila hum dono ne rakha,

Na tumne bada ban na chaha na mene,

Fir ab yeh kaisa dikhava,

Ab toh mujhe tumhe maaf karna hee padega

Akhir tumne apna ek waada nibhaya,

Jeete ji nahi, tumne meri maut pe mere liye

Apne ashq bahaye or keemti waqt gavaya"

6. Dying in Arms of Stranger

When you visit my city, my birthplace
Go to the street, ask my name
Ask my name from my home and burning flame
Back then I was quite popular
Had, stardom-like celebrities, not exact but quite similar
Don't forget to visit the nearby shop
That old man with the long beard
Is he still doing the job?
Visit the nearby park, it is lush green there
Or finding even grass is rare?
Take out my journal and bury it under the mango tree,
I plea
Let my thoughts and writings become ashes,
Who can bring the atmosphere to my city near my graveyard
Not even any cash or the memory of flashes
I might not be able to visit my city again,
So,
Ask my city to open its arms and let me be part of its Memory Lane.

Resourced : Google

7. Wo Mera Apna Shehar

Jeete ji tumare ahmiyat nahi thee
Aaj janaja jab dusre shehar ki gali se nikala
Tab har lamha tumare hawao mein bitaya hua
Aankho k saamne se gujarte huye nikala
Jab tak tumare ghar mein thee
Toh maano mujhse badi hasti koi nahi thee
Iss shehar mein toh mujhe koi janta tak nahi
Ab mumkin nahi mein apne do pero pe wapas aa paau
Par bejaan, raakh ya khaak jaise bhi aau,
Apne baahon mein bhar lena
Aee mere shehar mujhe bhi apne ek bache ki tarah
Apni kahani kisso mein thodi si jagah dedena!

"Mein kahi bhi tha,

Tumara aks humesha mere saath tha,

Shaksiyat meri kuch bhi thee,

Kaam or naam mera kuch bhi tha,

Par mein jahan bhi se bhi gujara

Sirf tumare naam se jana jaata raha - Jaipur!"

8. Your Remembrance

How do you want the world to remember you
A hero or has no clue
Do you want them to call you a legend after your death
Or forget in a few seconds after the last breath
But have you worked hard to fulfill this wish
Of remembering you as disguise or bliss
Do you want your body scent should flow in the air or your personality aroma to do all the magic?
Should we consider you lucky
Or your death as tragic
Oh dear friend, why haven't you mentioned your end,
I remember you said you have everything planned
You were even confident the way you will die,
I knew it was not your hand, you just denied
Well, your mother remembers you as the best child
Your father's emotions are still unwielded
Your pet lost its joy,
For some, you have become the long-forgotten memory
For some, you still live in their heart like the love that they carry
Goodbye, hope you are not planning your life after death, my friend it's time to take a rest!

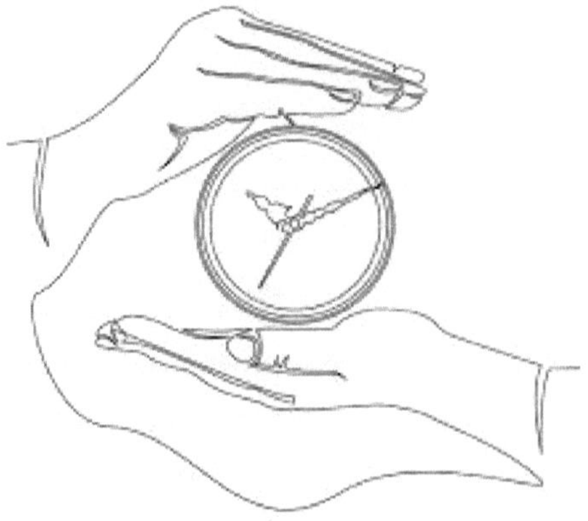

Resourced : Google

9. Kaisi Yaad Banenge Hum

Agar mein kahu ki mujhe yaad hee mat rakhna
Na ache mein na bure mein
Mere jaate hee, beete huye kal ki tarah bhula dena
Par shayad yeh mumkin nahi hoga
Insaan thee na, mere astitav ka darpan tumare yaadon mein jarur hoga
Par mujhe kaha pata hai
Mere insaniyat ki khushboo mere jaane k baad tak bhi mehakegi,
Ya bas logo ki bheed mein khoke khatam hojaygi
Haa mana mein kaha karta tha ki mujhe pata hai kab kya hoga,
Par maut toh wahi hai na jo jindagi ko deti hai dhoka
Umeed hai, Maa mujhe aaj bhi unka sabse acha bacha kehti hogi
Par Papa ne aaj bhi aankhein num karne se phele das dafa sochi hogi
Or jo mujhe jaan se bhi pyara tha mere paaltu kutta
Jeete ji usne mujhe kabhi akela mehsoos nahi hone diya,
Magar shayad mein uska yeh karz kabhi na chuka paya
Haa kissi ko mera acha yaad hai,
Kissi ko bura,
Mein jaise bhi yaad hu,

Mujhe nahi jaan na
Mene ek achi jindagi jee hai,
Or ab samay hai mere aram ka!

"Beete huye kal aaj or aane waale kal

Se mujhe rahat mil gayi,

Jiss maut ko sochne se bhi darta tha

Aaj wo meri asliyat ban gayi"

10. Thought For After Death

Now, it's time to go
I am afraid without me how things will go!
Listen, Listen
I can't stay anymore,
It's my time to leave
As all the five elements are ready to conceive me
I don't want to go
But can't stay as my death is calling me
Time to travel solo
Stay strong the path is wide and shallow
I might not be there physically
You will surely feel my energy flow
Hope you'll smile after my demise
As I am not your beginning or end
Just your Dear Friend
Whether my children or grandchildren gonna remember me
Or I will be lost in the divine tranquility
I have lived my life enough
Where I saw the pain, suffering, joy, and love
I am happy with the way the story of my life is ending

Still wondering, if is there any task that is still pending
I know the pain of demise is unbearable for few
I ensure things will be as normal as it was
Things will be tough, till the last but only for few
You gonna be fine, let me enjoy my red wine
Ahhh! I am dead
No stress of past, present and future
Raise the toast,
I am not believing in the "life after death" rumor.

Resourced : Google

11. Aisa Kyu Ho Raha Hai?

Yeh moh kyu mujhe abhi bhi bhande huye hai,
Akhri saans darwaje pe dastak de rahi hai
Maut aagayi par chinta toh dekho mujhe kal ki aaj bhi sata rahi hai
Maano mere jaane k baad yeh samay ruk jayga
Or tumari jindagi tham jaygi!
Haan, bhari puri jindagi jee hai mene
Apne bacho k saath or unke bacho k saath khela hu mein
Pata nahi wo mujhe kabhi yaad rakhenge ya nahi
Jo bhi hai, jaisa bhi mene apni jindagi jee li hai
Or ab meri kahani khatam hogayi hai
Chalo tum dekho ab mere jaane k baad kya hoga
Jo bhi hoga manjur-e-khuda hoga!

"Maut agayi pass mein moh abhi bhi nahi jaa raha,

Mere marne k baad mere apno ka kya hoga,

Yeh kaisa dar hai sata raha?

Are, chod de apne kal hone na hone ki chinta,

Maut ko gale laga or ab bas chain ki neend soja

Mein bas apne aapko yeh samjha raha"

12. Death Of A Soilder

I have chosen the way I will die
Still, I was not 100 per cent sure, Sigh!
The day I saw the dream of serving my nation
My mother took a deep breath filled with stress and tension
She knew I had chosen the best way to serve society
But somewhere, she knew the ground reality
Today, I am lying in the arms of my motherland
No arms are covering me with two hands
But, this death looks much more grand
As, I will be covered with my national flag
The whole country will mourn my death,
However, it is still time to celebrate
I was on a mission, killed our enemies
And chose the process of final rights
Dear wife, your husband died in the war
They call me a martyr, but you are my lioness time to roar
Dear child, you never saw me in real
I was going to visit you this summer,
But, I think this way is more ideal
Dear parents, I can't even think of the pain you are going through
You are the war child parents, just to know
With your blessings, I fulfilled my purpose of serving the nation

Time to say goodbye,

Thank You for the blessings and such honoured cremation.

Resourced : Google

13. Ek Maut Aisi Bhi

Wo kehte hai na -
"ek sipahi kafan toh uss din hee pehan leta hai jab wo sipahi bane ka sapna dekhta hai"
Toh kuch waisa hee hai,
Maut toh meri aaj huyi hai,
Kafan pehne toh mein barso se ghoom raha hu,
Jiss din desh k liye jindagi jeene ka socha tha
Uss din apne or apno k liye jeena bhul chuka tha
Par mere liye garv ki baat hai ki,
Mein shaeed k naam se jana jaunga
Jissne dushmano ko harake veergati prapti ki,
Tum ek sherni ho isliye hee toh tumne mujhe chunna,
Yeh jaante huye bhi ki mein aaj hu or kal nahi
Or suno mere bache se kehna, mein usse dekhna chahta tha
Par shayad uska mujhe aise hee dekhna sabse sahi tha
Or Ma-papa mein aapki halat soch bhi nahi sakta,
Par jinhone apna bacha desh ko pehle hee dediya tha,
Unki taakat ka toh mein andaja hee nahi laga sakta
Shukr guzar hu mein ki mujhe apne desh ki maati mein maut milli
Or kal tak jo sirf ek sipahi k naam se jana jaata tha,
Usse uski maut ne virgati dedi!

"Mein veer tha or veer k naam se jana jaunga,

Iss maati ka karz na mein utaar paunga,

Aee vatan tu mere liye mere apno se bhi upar hai,

Mein maut k baad bhi yahi geet gaunga!"

Treat For The Shayari Lovers

Wo yaad tak rakh na sake meri apne pass,
Jo mere saya bane ka wada kiye karte theh
Wo janaje pe toh mere aa na sake,
Jo tere bin mar kaise jeeyenge aisi baatein kiya karte theh

Jindagi ko kai rango mein dekha hai mene,
Kabhi Khushi, Kabhi Gum, Kabhi Saadgi
or Kabhi Cham-Cham

Be-khauf jeeta raha,

Be-khayal aage badhta raha,

Be-kadar logo ki taraf raha,

Be-khayali mein afsane sunata raha,

Or Be-waqt duniya se chal diya

Jindagi kuch aisi nikal, jindagi kuch waisi nikali

Jissne jaise dekha, jiya or mana jindagi ko,

Unki asal mein jindagi waisi nikali

Mana kissi ne sikhaya hai ki,
sukh mein araam milta hai,
Dukh mein ajaab milta hai,
Par kissi ne yeh bhi toh kaha tha
Akele sukh bhi bura lagta hai,
Or apno k saath dukh kaha poora lagta hai

Kissi ne apni jindagi -
lamho mein ginayi,
kissi ne yaadon mein,
kissi ne logo mein,
kissi ne iraado mein,
kissi ne kamayi mein,
kissi ne kissi ki judaai mein,
Kissi ne khwabon mein,
Kissi ne hakkikat mein,
Or fir asal mein,
Usne ginaayi,
Jisski jindagi rahi
Inn sabhi baaton mein

9 798889 862383

Printed by Libri Plureos GmbH in Hamburg, Germany